ACTIVITY BOOK FOR STRONG AND CONFIDENT GIRLS

CONFIDENT ME!

FROM THE BEST SELLING SISTER TO SISTER SERIES

Dr. Marilou Ryder & Jessica Thompson

CONFIDENT ME!

COPYRIGHT ©2023 Marilou Ryder and Jessica Thompson

All rights reserved: No part of this publication may be reproduced or transmitted in any form or by any means, mechanical, or electronic, including photocopying and recording or by an information storage and retrieval system without permission in writing from the authors (except by a reviewer, who may quote brief passages).

ISBN: 979-8-9870551-3-7

Publicity Rights

For information on publicity, author interview, presentation, or subsidiary rights, contact; Dr. Marilou Ryder: drmlr@yahoo.com |760.900.0556

Jessica Thompson: rthompson22@comcast.net | 978.879.9288

Printed in the United States of America

Delmar Publishing, Huntington Beach, CA 92648

Dear Parents and Guardians,

Thank you so much for choosing CONFIDENT ME! – the perfect activity book for that special girl in your life. We're all about nurturing young girls' confidence and self-advocacy, which are like superpowers that grow stronger with practice. Our book is jam-packed with fun exercises designed to boost confidence and self-awareness, covering all sorts of exciting life topics.

CONFIDENT ME! is tailor-made for awesome 5-12-year-olds, providing not just entertainment but also some serious developmental value. Dive into these exercises together and watch her journey toward self-assurance take off!

In today's ever-changing world, it's crucial to equip our young ones with the right tools and mindset to handle challenges, boost self-esteem, and become confident, strong individuals. "Confident Me" isn't just any old activity book; it's a carefully crafted guide that instills resilience, self-assuredness, and a super positive self-image in our precious girls.

As parents, you're well aware of how childhood challenges can impact self-esteem, and that's where our book comes in. It provides an interactive platform for self-empowerment, promoting positive self-talk and self-care through loads of engaging activities.

CONFIDENT ME! is all about uplifting messages and empowering illustrations, encouraging girls to celebrate their strengths and embrace their uniqueness. Through coloring and activities, your child will pick up crucial self-care practices that'll serve her well in life.

So, here's our invitation: Let's embark on this awesome journey of self-discovery and growth together! Let's inspire our girls to become the confident, resilient, and empowered leaders of tomorrow. We hope you enjoy CONFIDENT ME! as much as we enjoyed creating it, and that it fills your days with joy and positivity!

Best of Luck,
Marilou Ryder and Jessica Thompson

THIS BOOK

Belongs To:

Self Check-In

TODAY I AM FEELING

I DESERVE TO FEEL

I'M GRATEFUL FOR

What is CONFIDENCE?

- I feel liked and accepted.
- I think good things about myself.
- I am proud of what I can do.
- I can speak up for myself.

What is CONFIDENCE?

I like myself.

I always do my best.

I try new things.

Good Stuff

Everyone has something that they are good at. Are you good at sports, music or science? What do you like to do? What are you doing when people say, "Oh I like that!" Think of some thing that you are good at.

At home I am good at....

At school I am good at....

With my friends I am good at....

CHECKLIST
for Confidence ✓

	I'M GOOD AT THIS	I'M OK AT THIS	STILL WORKING ON THIS
I am always on time for any event.			
I know when it's my turn to speak up.			
I work at keeping friendships.			

My New Confidence Goal is ...

BE MY BEST SELF ON A
GOOD DAY

WHAT ARE WAYS I KEEP MY BODY HEALTHY?

1. _____

2. _____

3. _____

NOTES

_____
_____
_____

Sharp Thinker

Word Search

```
D G F C F U C V A O C M H Q S
P T R U L E T D R X O S H V E
R L X K X M Q A Q C I L J H F
O O D Z L E M P O W E R J J F
U X C G P X T V X S I F O H Q
D X O P A Z D N Y Z W Z M S R
C A N D T L U J V K D L Y L V
M X F S I P M T O B C Q J W O
W H I K E O M K I D X B Y S D
X P D W N S V W C G Y K N T A
K R E M C I Q G E S F U X R N
T Y N U E T S M A R T H H O V
X W C J G I Y P L O V E D N A
A P E O S V I U G R O P U G Y
K P M W H E J Y R C L T H S R
```

Confidence	**Empower**	**Loved**
Patience	**Strong**	**Proud**
Positive	**Smart**	**Voice**

FINISH DRAWING THE
CONFIDENT GIRL

Color it in

EVERY DAY

IS A FRESH START

I'M A WANNA BEE

When you find out what's important to you it lets you make changes that can improve your life. Take some time to think about the areas below and circle the number of bees according to how important they are to you. The more bees circled, the more important!

JOINING A CLUB
PLAYING SPORTS
A BEST FRIEND
HAVING FRIENDS
BEING THE BEST
TELLING THE TRUTH
WINNING
BEING PERFECT
BEING ON TIME
BEING SAFE
LOOKING PRETTY

KEEPING A SECRET
HELPING A FRIEND
KNOWING THE ANSWER
BEING GOOD AT SCIENCE
BEING GOOD AT MATH
SPEAKING UP
BEING LIKED
EATING HEALTHY
EXERCISING
BEING THE LEADER
WATCHING TV
SOCIAL MEDIA
READING BOOKS
HELPING A FRIEND

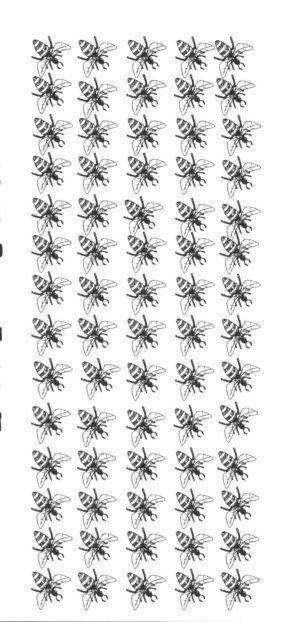

Based on your score, write down a few WANNA BEE changes you might WANNA make.

CONFIDENCE
QUIZ

Savannah received a compliment about her adorable hair style. She says ...

A) I wish I had blonde hair

B) Thank you

C) It was my Mom's idea

THE ANSWER PLEASE

Answer B: You are taught to say 'thank you' when someone gives you a cookie. Don't hide your light under a cloud. Learn to accept praise for yourself. Try not to make excuses. Learn to say a simple THANK YOU.

Make it Happen

Goals are all the things you want to accomplish in your life. They can be large and challenging goals, or they can be smaller and more personal. When a person writes down a goal, it usually gets accomplished and their confidence soars. Write down three goals that you would like to accomplish this month.

My Goals

1.

2.

3.

BRAIN TEASER

A sharp, healthy brain has a positive impact on your mind and body. A sharp mind can make you more confident in everything you do.

CAN YOU SPOT 6 DIFFERENCES

CHECKLIST
for Confidence ✓

	I'M GOOD AT THIS	I'M OK AT THIS	STILL WORKING ON THIS
I stand up tall with good posture.	☐	☐	☐
I am a good listener.	☐	☐	☐
I do something to exercise my mind every day.	☐	☐	☐

My New Confidence Goal is...

BE MY BEST SELF ON A
GOOD DAY

WHAT ARE WAYS I KEEP MY MIND HEALTHY?

1. _____
_____
_____

2. _____
_____
_____

3. _____
_____

NOTES
_____
_____
_____

EMPOWERMENT SCRABBLE

How many confidence words can you make using the letters below?

e	b	o	l
r	n	v	y
p	a	i	t
m	o	c	d

_____   _____

_____   _____

_____   _____

Tag your friend and see who gets the most!

FINISH DRAWING THE CONFIDENT GIRL

MIXED EMOTIONS

Being able to tell what emotion a person is feeling is important when dealing with friends and adults in your life. Facial expressions are probably the most important signal of an emotion because they tell us how a person is feeling and how they might act toward you.

DRAW THE EMOTION TO EACH FACE

surprised

shy

tired

happy

DEAR DIARY

Writing in a diary is a lot like journaling. When you write down your thoughts and feelings you begin to understand them more clearly. The beauty of journaling is that there's no right or wrong way to do it. It's a deeply personal experience that can take many forms. Use the next few pages to begin writing down some of your thoughts and feelings.

Today I was so proud of myself for...

I was even able to ..

I am so excited for...

I think I will...

Tomorrow I am going to...

After I finish I am going to start...

At this moment I feel so good about...

When I'm happy I can...

Today I was really good at...

I believe that I can....

Today in school I...

It made me feel...

I think I learned...

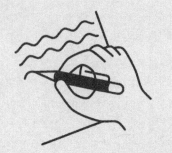

Someone at school is...

I'm not sure but I think I should...

Anytime this happens I always...

Today I tried so hard at...

I think it's crazy how......

I believe I could...

CONFIDENCE QUIZ

A few girls at school keep calling your classmate 'chubby' and you know it hurts her feelings. You…

A) Feel sorry for her

B) Tell your Mom

C) Speak up and tell the girls to stop

THE ANSWER PLEASE

Answer C: While telling your parents or a teacher is a good solution, the best tactic is to speak up when the bullying is happening. Be bold and tell the girls to stop. Speak up when you think something is wrong or don't agree with it.

CONFIDENT VIBES

The brain can be tricky. This means that on any given day it tends to hear five negative messages for each positive one received. Start sending positive vibes to your brain every day to tell it you are amazing and special. Connect at least five words that describe your confidence level right now!

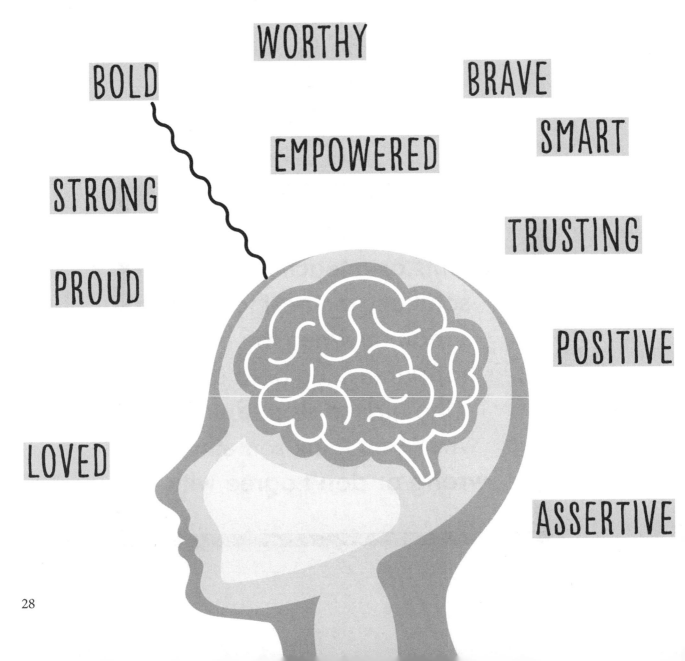

WORTHY
BOLD
BRAVE
SMART
EMPOWERED
STRONG
TRUSTING
PROUD
POSITIVE
LOVED
ASSERTIVE

CHECKLIST
for Confidence ✓

	I'M GOOD AT THIS	I'M OK AT THIS	STILL WORKING ON THIS
I belong to a club or sport at school.			
I get a good night's sleep.			
I am not afraid to try new things.			

My New Confidence Goal is...

BE MY BEST SELF ON A
GOOD DAY

HOW DO I MAKE MYSELF HAPPY?

1. _____
   _____
   _____
2. _____
   _____
   _____
3. _____
   _____

NOTES

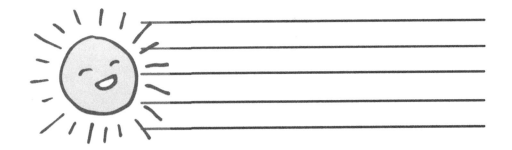

FINISH DRAWING THE CONFIDENT GIRL

PERSONAL PASSWORDS

Circle Your Password to Confidence

LEADER

A. Something you climb.
B. A person who is confident and takes charge.
C. Something found inside a pencil.

A. Having value and importance.
B. A butterscotch candy.
C. A coat you wear during cold weather.

WORTHY

EMPOWER

A. An electrical plant.
B. Having the authority or power to do something.
C. A very large government.

ANSWERS: Leader (b); Worthy (a); Empower (b)

WHAT CAN I BE FROM A - Z

CIRCLE CAREERS THAT YOU COULD IMAGINE IN YOUR FUTURE

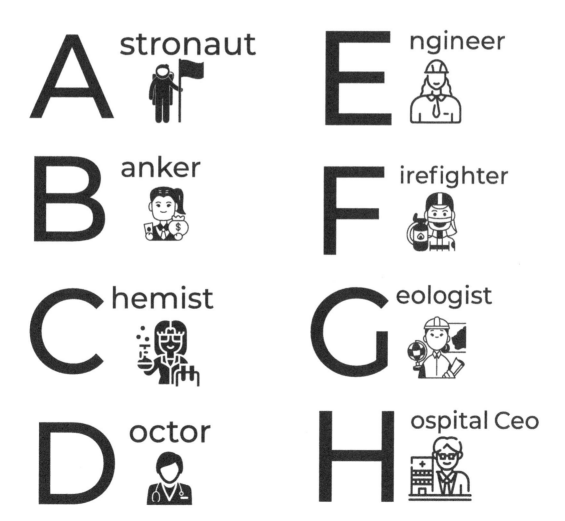

CIRCLE CAREERS THAT YOU COULD IMAGINE IN YOUR FUTURE

Interpreter

News Reporter

Judge

Orthodontist

Karate Instructor

Pilot

Lawyer

Quality Controller

Meteorologist

Radiologist

CIRCLE CAREERS THAT YOU COULD IMAGINE IN YOUR FUTURE

Surgeon

Web Designer

Therapist

Xenobotanist

Ultra Sound Specialist

Yoga Teacher

Veterinarian

Zoologist

BRAIN TEASER

A sharp, healthy brain has a positive impact on your mind and body. A sharp mind can make you more confident in everything you do.

CAN YOU SPOT 6 DIFFERENCES

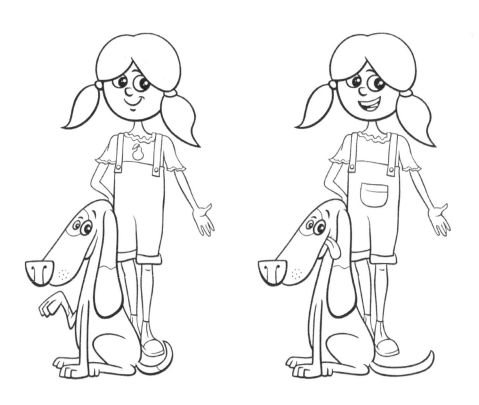

LET'S PLAY TIC TAC TOE

Put a star on squares that show confidence.

Ask why I'm not in a higer math group	Look at the floor when asked a question	Hide my face in my hoodie
Be the first to say 'hi'	Be first to help a teacher	Laugh at someone who gives a wrong answer
Make fun of my friend	Sit in the front row	Always took up

ACTS OF KINDNESS

Performing acts of kindness releases a feel-good chemical in your brain which increases self-esteem and can lift your mood.

LIST THREE THINGS YOU CAN DO TO BE KIND

1 _____

2 _____

3 _____

PERSONAL PASSWORDS

Circle Your Password to Confidence

VISION
A. Preparing for the future.
B. A pair of eyeglasses.
C. The latest TV channel.

SUCCESS
A. Another section in a book.
B. A very nutritious squash.
C. A good result from working hard.

CHALLENGE
A. A spaceship.
B. The edge of a cliff.
C. To question the truth of something.

ANSWERS: Vision (a); Success (c); Challenge (c)

BE MY BEST SELF ON A
GOOD DAY

WHAT DO I DO TO HELP OTHERS?

1. _____

2. _____

3. _____

NOTES

_____

SLEEPING BEAUTY

Even though Mom and Dad are right down the hall, sometimes you are still afraid of having a bad dream. Draw your dream fears below, talk about them with Mom or Dad and then cross them out!

DREAM GIRL

What are your dreams for the future? One day you will be all grown up and wish you could be right back where you are now. For now, just enjoy being little and dream up all of the things you want to do with your life.

CONFIDENCE QUIZ

You have a project that's due tomorrow, but your friends want you to go to the movies. You...

A) Blow off the project and go to the movie because friends are important.

B) Rush through the project so you can do both.

C) Thank your friends but tell them you need to stay home to complete your project.

THE ANSWER PLEASE

Answer C: Why does it always seem like everything happens all at once? While friends are important they will be there tomorrow but your project won't unless you complete it on time!

There are so many different career options now for females. Find all the hidden careers in this word search. When circling each career ask yourself, "Would this be a career I should learn more about?"

I COULD BE A....

S	C	A	R	P	E	N	T	E	R	R	T	D	D
A	T	S	I	G	O	L	O	R	E	T	E	M	O
R	N	T	R	T	N	O	E	G	R	U	S	S	C
C	A	R	P	D	O	E	T	E	L	H	T	A	T
H	I	P	J	H	E	L	T	S	I	T	R	A	O
I	C	B	W	O	A	N	I	C	N	C	L	T	R
T	I	A	E	T	U	R	T	P	E	U	A	S	O
E	R	N	L	H	T	R	M	I	R	O	R	R	S
C	T	K	D	I	I	M	N	A	S	R	A	S	S
T	C	E	E	E	C	I	E	A	C	T	O	I	E
O	E	R	R	E	T	I	R	W	L	I	P	R	F
C	L	H	R	E	T	N	I	A	P	I	S	T	O
R	E	T	S	I	T	N	E	I	C	S	S	T	R
T	E	R	R	P	R	E	S	I	D	E	N	T	P

PHARMACIST
PILOT
WELDER
PRESIDENT
SCIENTIST
DOCTOR
SURGEON
BANKER
CARPENTER
NURSE
ARCHITECT
ATHLETE
ELECTRICIAN
JOURNALIST
PAINTER
DENTIST
CEO
PROFESSOR
WRITER
ARTIST

Play this puzzle online at : https://thewordsearch.com/puzzle/5480914/

LET'S PLAY TIC TAC TOE

Put a star on squares that show confidence.

Sit in the front row	Be quiet all the time	Sit in the back row
Be proud of an **A+**	Be first to raise my hand	Roll my eyes at my friend
Love myself	Talk when my teacher is talking	Say thank you

CHECKLIST
for Confidence ✓

	I'M GOOD AT THIS	I'M OK AT THIS	STILL WORKING ON THIS
I am good at math and science.			
I try to learn from my mistakes.			
I stick with a project until it's finished.			

My New Confidence Goal is ...

Color it in

LOVE YOURSELF FIRST

PERSONAL PASSWORDS

Circle Your Password to Confidence

MENTOR
A. Candy that tastes like peppermint.
B. When you mean to do something.
C. A trusted counselor or guide.

A. Rating something or someone for its worth.
B. A coupon or stamp.
C. The hairpiece a bride wears.

A. A very strong fence.
B. Having faith in oneself and one's power.
C. Something solid and deep.

ANSWERS: Mentor (c) Value; (a); Confidence (B)

Draw the emotion

LEARN THE
POWER POSE

The power pose can do wonders for improving your self-confidence. It is best performed anytime you feel unsure about yourself. Known as the 'superhero pose' it involves standing like a superhero. You may begin to feel the effects after as little as 2 minutes.

TRY THESE STEPS

1. CHIN UP

2. ROLL SHOULDERS BACK

3. HANDS ON HIP

4. LEGS HIP LENGTH APART ON THE GROUND

FINISH DRAWING THE CONFIDENT GIRL

PERSONAL PASSWORDS

Circle Your Password to Confidence

PASSION

A. Having a powerful emotion or feeling for something.
B. A fruit punch.
C. A shade of purple.

ACHIEVEMENT

A. When everyone agrees.
B. A substance to pave roads.
C. When you do something successfully using your own effort or skiils.

RESPONSIBLE

A. Answering your phone as soon as possible.
B. Doing something real fast.
C. Being trusted and relied on for important duties.

ANSWERS: Passion (a) Achievement (c) Responsible (c)

BE MY BEST SELF ON A
GOOD DAY

1. WHAT ARE SOME GROUPS AND CLUBS I CAN JOIN AT SCHOOL?

_____

_____

2. WHO DO I TELL TO LET THEM KNOW WHEN I'M NOT HAPPY?

_____

_____

3. WHO CAN I GO TO AT SCHOOL IF I NEED HELP?

_____

_____

NOTES

_____

_____

_____

I DID THAT!

Whenever you are low on confidence it always helps to make a list of your latest accomplishments. Write an accomplishment in each drawing below and watch your confidence soar!

Find all the words that are connected with CONFIDENCE. When circling each word, think how it relates to being a confident girl!

CONNECTED TO CONFIDENCE

H	L	G	O	A	L	S	H	Y	B	B	O	H	A
R	E	S	P	E	C	T	S	U	C	C	E	S	S
L	Y	A	C	H	I	E	V	E	M	E	N	T	E
S	L	T	L	E	T	H	L	R	L	S	E	C	L
P	H	E	I	T	B	T	H	U	I	S	F	E	B
O	E	N	E	N	H	H	R	S	S	T	R	M	I
R	W	C	D	E	G	Y	N	O	T	R	I	E	S
T	F	O	E	E	X	I	A	P	E	O	E	N	N
S	A	U	R	O	V	E	D	M	N	N	N	T	O
O	I	R	H	T	E	Y	R	O	P	G	D	O	P
H	T	A	M	T	H	C	I	C	R	R	S	R	S
R	G	G	N	O	S	Y	S	C	I	E	N	C	E
E	H	E	Y	S	B	U	L	C	D	S	M	S	R
R	L	E	A	D	E	R	E	Y	E	C	E	L	R

ACHIEVEMENT
HEALTHY
DIGNITY
COMPOSURE
HOBBY
PRIDE
LEADER
SPORTS
ENCOURAGE
GOALS
MATH
SCIENCE
RESPONSIBLE
SUCCESS
LISTEN
RESPECT
STRONG
CLUBS
MENTOR
FRIENDS
WORTHY
EXERCISE

Play this puzzle online at : https://thewordsearch.com/puzzle/5482982/

LOV IN' LIFE

Knowing what you LOVE in life helps to define your values and makes you special and unique. Write what you LOVE in the hearts for each category.

Books you loved reading

Movie you love to watch over and over

Foods that make you happy

Sport you love to play

Friends you love to be with

You just love this holiday

LOV IN' LIFE

What do you love about being a girl?

What do you love about yourself?

What recording artist do you love?

What do you love about your best friend?

What ice cream flavor do you love the most?

What time of day do you love the most?

What TV show do you love watching?

What would you love to finish?

CONFIDENCE QUIZ

Your best friend tells you that she doesn't like the new sweater you are wearing. You...

A) Agree with her because you want her to like you.

B) Tell her you like the sweater because that's why you bought it.

C) Get upset with her and tell her you don't like her new shoes.

THE ANSWER PLEASE

Answer B: You want your friends to like you and your style but when they don't it shouldn't bother you. Growing up and having confidence is all about liking yourself and who you are!

EMOTIONAL MIX & MATCH

Emotional awareness, or the ability to understand feelings, will help you succeed when communicating with other people. If you notice the emotions of other people and the way they are feeling you can communicate better.

CONNECT AN EMOTION TO THE FACE

- DISAPPOINTED
- SILLY
- PASSIONATE
- PROUD
- AMUSED
- DOUBTFUL
- POSITIVE
- SAD
- ANNOYED
- LOVED

FINISH DRAWING THE CONFIDENT GIRL

PERSONAL PASSWORDS

Circle Your Password to Confidence

VOICE
- A. Speakers made for underwater.
- B. A hit movie.
- C. The right to express your opinion and make a difference.

EDUCATION
- A. A type of school or church.
- B. A song by the Beatles.
- C. Knowledge, skills, and development gained from study or practice.

GOAL
- A. Something made of metal.
- B. An award you receive at the end of a game.
- C. A target you are trying to reach or achieve.

ANSWERS: Voice (c) Education (c) Goal (c)

Color it in

POSITIVE VIBES ONLY

BRAIN TEASER

A sharp, healthy brain has a positive impact on your mind and body. A sharp mind can make you more confident in everything you do.

affirmations
af·firm·a·tions [noun]

Positive statements that you repeat to yourself over and over again. They are the perfect way to remind your mind of all the things you like about yourself and it is where self-love starts.

Create Your Own
AFFIRMATIONS

PERSONAL PASSWORDS

Circle Your Password to Confidence

BRAVE
A. One of the greatest movies ever made.
B. A professional football team.
C. When one is willing to do things that are difficult and not be afraid.

ENCOURAGE
A. To give someone support, courage or hope.
B. When someone gets very mad.
C. A beautiful flower arrangement.

PROUD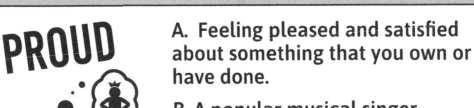
A. Feeling pleased and satisfied about something that you own or have done.
B. A popular musical singer.
C. A famous tee shirt brand.

ANSWERS: Brave (c) Encourage (a) Proud (a)

CONFIDENCE CHECK

COLOR THE FACE THAT YOU FEEL NOW

Made in the USA
Middletown, DE
06 January 2025

68965179R00044